ALL THE EYES THAT I HAVE OPENED

FRANCA MANCINELLI

translated by John Taylor

BSE Books are distributed by
  Small Press Distribution
  1341 Seventh Street
  Berkeley, CA 94710
  orders@spdbooks.org | www.spdbooks.org
  1-800-869-7553

BSE Books can also be purchased at
www.blacksquareeditions.org and www.hyperallergic.com

Contributions to BSE can be made to
  Off the Park Press, Inc.
  c/o Margaret Galey
  PO Box 1401
  Lexington, KY 40588
  (Please make checks payable to Off the Park Press, Inc.)

To contact the Press please write:
  Black Square Editions
  1200 Broadway, Suite 3C
  New York, NY 10001

An imprint of Off the Park Press, Inc. Member of CLMP.

Publisher: John Yau
Editors: Ronna Lebo and Boni Joi
Production Manager: Margaret Galey
Design & composition: Shanna Compton

Cover art: "Saint Lucy" (detail) by Francesco del Cossa, c. 1473/1474, tempera on poplar panel, Samuel H. Kress Collection, National Gallery of Art, Washington, DC. Courtesy National Gallery of Art, Washington.

CONTENTS

SPECCHIO RICURVO / CURVED MIRROR

TO THE TINY BRONZE OFFERING BEARERS FROM MOUNT TITANO

DECEMBER 13TH

From Pain to Possibilities of Vision: New Poems by Franca Mancinelli

When I read Franca Mancinelli's poetry, when I translate it, I am brought face to face with this question: Can something positive be drawn out of a negative experience—from psychic wounds, from loss or abandonment, from an unwanted state of homelessness, even from ruins and destruction? In short, can "pain" be turned into a "possibility of vision," as she phrases it? It is this existential question that stands out in this new collection, and it builds into a theme that is also a movement, in the musical sense of the term, appearing and reappearing, indeed structuring the book as one section or sequence leads to, and dialogues with, the next one. Readers of *The Little Book of Passage* and *At an Hour's Sleep from Here* (which gathers her first two books, *Mala Kruna* and *Mother Dough*), not to mention her collection of prose narratives and personal essays, *The Butterfly Cemetery*, know that her grappling with this issue stems from deep necessities. And if we listen attentively to her, this is because her carefully considered and ever-compelling poetic responses, be they expressed in the first or second person singular, always go beyond the poet's self and concern us directly.

She begins with a concrete fact or happenstance, which she has experienced or witnessed, and then, with penetrating insight and exacting stylistic concision, she distills the essence—be it a state of mind and body or an enigma of our being-in-the-cosmos—that we can no longer avoid because it is also ours or can become ours.

The title of this new volume, *All the Eyes that I Have Opened*, is intimately related to this creative quest of sight and insight, of affirmation and openness, of building and rebuilding in the face of various kinds of blinding, negation, closure, and unbuilding. As an italicized distich in one of her poems reveals, the underlying image is that of a tree:

> *all the eyes that I have opened*
> *are the branches that I have lost.*

When a branch is removed—broken off by chance or sawed off intentionally—an "eye" remains. There is great pain, but this new "eye" can enable one to see something else, or differently. Potentially, a positive transformation can take place. As on a maimed tree trunk, an eye has opened on the body, as it were. Perhaps this eye still has scabs and scars, trickles of sap or blood, bruises and jagged edges—the fragmentary style of these poems reflect this, and with masterful craftsmanship—but unexpected horizons, and previously unnoticed presences, benevolent and nearby, have now come into sight. In her poetic prose text "An Act of Inner Self-Surgery" (*The Butterfly Cemetery*), Mancinelli explains how she came up with this title or, rather, how it came to her:

> Once a few years ago in a woods in the Apennines, I was
> walking for hours, full of inner devastation, entrusting my

sorrow to every footstep, listening to the light within the foliage of the trees, to disperse the circles of my torment like water enveloping a smooth boulder fallen to the bottom. When suddenly a tree with a very scarred trunk came to meet me. *All the eyes that I have opened are the branches that I have lost*—it said to me. Its sparse foliage opened out high, far above my eyes. You could read in its bark the history of cuts and amputations, healed and transformed into growth, obedient to light, beyond all obstacles. I continued to walk with this voice that had been articulated in me, and one clear image: there are losses that you can weep over with all your tears, fight with every effort, yet they are necessary. We would give our whole life so that they won't happen, yet they are guiding our sap towards the shape and the place that belongs to it.

As she works through a painful severing and thereby acquires a deeper awareness and a new outlook (in the literal sense), Mancinelli is thus guided or counseled by this and other "master trees" (as she calls them). Such trees, as well as other natural elements invoked by Mancinelli in what she calls her "affective botany," can teach us how to face up to pain and wounds and thus how to keep standing. In Italian, "alberi maestri" also means the "mainmasts" of a ship; in English, we can also think of a related, though different, nautical term that has a figurative meaning: "mainstays." Relying on the age-old strength and guiding "mast-like" qualities of the trees, Mancinelli thus confronts head-on the negative factor: the harmfulness, the noxiousness, the threats to her—and, more generally, to our—well-being or personhood. In other words, her writing seeks to touch, to embrace, to take root in, to grow from, whatever can teach us, with a wisdom that we alone cannot muster, about disappointment, damage, and tragedy; she seeks sources that refresh and re-nourish, origins that restore and cure, or, to paraphrase one poem here, she "points" her eyes so that her "area" or "circle of life" will be "rounded off." Here, "point" is a verb that indicates aiming exactly (which is another theme for her, that of seeing precisely), whereas the noun "point," in its acceptation as a point of convergence, also crops up in poems where it suggests an "initial" or—to use an apt archaic word—"originary" locus at which all the crucial elements have gathered and from which all things are generated:

> it has happened, stay: in the dark
> hollow like a uterus, dwell
>
> there is a point when life overturns
> becomes Morse code.

The reader of these succinct poems, such as the one just cited, might well have the impression that they are themselves "points" or, rather, "focal points" (to recall the photographic analogies sometimes employed by Mancinelli in this book). As her translator and reader, I often sense that by concentrating my attention on such fragments, I narrow in on something dense and compact— something indeed like a "point," even a "black hole," if this analogy is not too far-fetched—which, after a meditative moment, opens out for me into a vaster, multidimensional meaning. Like a "white hole"? In any case, the imagery of conception and pregnancy in the above poem releases—gives birth to, I could say—a cluster of significations that engage not only with the biological senses of coming into the world and being alive, but also with the coming into language—the Morse code—of our attempt to construct a meaning from them. Life itself can turn itself into a code that must be deciphered, into writing that must be read. And yet the "dark / hollow," likened to a uterus, might also be something else: a refuge, metaphorical or not, where one can find care and protection. As has been seen, Mancinelli often draws her similes and metaphors from natural elements such as animals, various types of vegetation, or landscape features. Moreover, in her poetic cosmos, everything is in movement, even in metamorphosis, and forms are never definite; they are heading towards new forms, their next forms. In their migration, identities open out, take on other configurations; bodies can come to have "an open texture," as a text in the last section, *Diary of Passage,* phrases it." The epigraph, which evokes "birds of passage" and thus implicitly alludes to the title *Diary of Passage,* states this:

> cannot scatter itself
> puts itself back together at every turn
> like a flock flying onwards.

In the epigraph, the grammatical subject is tellingly left un-specified. As a subset of this greater ensemble, human beings sim-ilarly fly onwards, leave their "contours"—as Mancinelli puts it in "a spoon in sleep," her well-known poem from *Mother Dough*—and evolve into other forms, joining along the way something greater. It is a matter of being liberated and liberating oneself. "Sometimes it's a storm, or a rock bumped into," observes the poet, "deviating the course. And you find yourself free." Of course, these "storms" and "rocks" are also the decisive negative events whose destructive energy the poet attempts to convert into a new possibility of vision. Apropos of this destructive energy, she recalls, in "An Act of Inner Self-Surgery," her encounter with the Hindi female deity Kali in Calcutta, during her stay there as the Chair Poet in residence. One of the oldest temples devoted to Kali, the goddess of destructive forces, the destroyer of evil who also bestows "moksha" or enlightenment and emancipation, and the symbol of a primordial "darkness" from which everything is born, was in fact located just over a kilometer from where she was staying. "The forces of destruction are to be honored," writes Mancinelli, and "honoring them means recognizing their power, their presence, yielding a space to them where they can receive our gaze, the gifts of every day." She adds:

> Otherwise they awaken, demand our tribute in blood. [. . .]. I met [Kali] last winter in Calcutta. [. . .] And I felt how vital it was to recognize that destructive charge which, left inside us, emerges in the other person to whom we lend the knife. While if we learn to welcome this charge, we can direct it towards whatever limits us, whatever blocks our way, illuminating parts of us that had remained dark and getting closer to what we are.

Another way of thinking about, in fact viewing, the multifaceted burgeoning effect in Mancinelli's poems is clarified by the vocabulary of photography. She occasionally adopts such terms, in her poems or when she is describing her poetics, underscoring the notion of a "darkroom" into which she withdraws to create, that is, to use darkness and specifically the negative—the negative experience—to recover the hidden or forgotten light and then to shape this light, by means of words, into a tool enabling a new kind of seeing. "Light," in this context, therefore means elucidation, lucidity, becoming enlightened to a greater extent than before, and thus passing out of the darkness, at least for a while. The act of writing, as Mancinelli conceives of it, takes her into her darkroom, a "place of the unknown, where [her] demons nestle [and her] most tenacious and impenetrable shadows [can be found]," as she has explained. It is as if the poet has intently focused on something (an event, another person), perhaps in the present, perhaps retrospectively, even prospectively; the snapshot is taken; and then, in the darkroom, the haunting polymorphic image emerges, perhaps years later, from her stylistic chemicals. The sequence "Darkroom," which tells of a relationship, could not be more explicit:

> in the first sequence, you laughed and talked into my ear.
> You didn't know you were inside the framing of the photo.

✳

> at this distance I can keep you in focus. You stand still,
> as in the first moments. Your ashes carried by the wind,
> into my darkroom.

Yet there is a broader perspective to this initially personal work of writing in the darkroom. Personal or particular elements in Mancinelli's writing always aim for multiplicity and universality. She likes to cite the Italian philosopher Giorgio Agamben's essay, "What is the Contemporary?" in which one who is "contemporary" is defined as "one who firmly keeps his gaze on his own time to perceive, not its light, but its darkness." "All eras," continues Agamben, "are obscure—dark—for those who experience contemporaneity.

One who is contemporary is precisely one who knows how to see this obscurity, who is able to write by dipping his pen into the obscurity of the present."

These and many other images in Mancinelli's poetry, be they based on light and darkness or on natural elements—and however otherwise different—often merge in their search for a "beginning" at which, if one reaches it after the devastation, one's own being can be re-founded, one's own body be acknowledged or "recognized"—another key term—in new ways. Recognition and acceptance are required for seeing again, from one's new "eye," once the "branch" has been lopped off. Note the use of "recognize" in these sentences from "Diary of Passage" and, once again, the potential conversion of "abandonment" into "restitution," which is also a kind of "new start":

> The ravens have come to leave you with a lesson. The most difficult one. Those black fruits on the branches, that unexpected presence. And suddenly the detachment, the emptiness that comes back clearly. You call it *abandonment*, try to recognize it as a *restitution*.

At such beginnings where "restitution" can take place—at vital sources of renewal and growth—one's place in the everyday world and in the cosmos can be reestablished or at least re-envisioned. The Italian noun "inizio" and the verb "iniziare," and their various synonyms, in fact appear quite often in this collection, in contexts suggesting that "starting over again" and recovering something "initial," primal, primordial (in the sense of fundamental and necessary), depends on accepting ruins, even death in both its literal meaning and its metaphorical extensions. "Deaths are time's beads," writes Mancinelli in one distich, "we go through them like a string." And these deaths of our self, of our identity, bear us forward into other forms and existences. In one revealing poem, a symbolic "burial" leads to a "beginning" that comprises being put into the earth's benevolent safekeeping. The poet's being, her body, and her hands that write, are now like "roots at work":

> burial. And beginning. I am potted
> and possessed. I live in the earth's
> safekeeping, with hands sunk
> like roots at work.

"Burial and beginning." Mancinelli likes to cite T. S. Eliot's notion from "East Coker." "In my beginning is my end," he writes, and then, at the end of the same poem, he inverts these opening lines by borrowing, and slightly adjusting, the motto that Mary Queen of Scots embroidered not long before her execution: "En ma Fin gît mon Commencement." For the French verb "gît," Eliot writes not "lies" (as in "here lies"), but rather "is": "In my end is my beginning." And even as the Anglo-American poet places "ends" and "beginnings" on the ontological level, Mancinelli's poems also engage with our being-in-the-cosmos and in addition—this is not necessarily within Eliot's scope—with the question of "how to live." In this regard, I cannot help but evoke one French and two French-language Swiss poets whom I have also extensively translated: Pierre-Albert Jourdan, Philippe Jaccottet, José-Flore Tappy. Like them, Mancinelli explores the ways in which we can better embrace our transitory human condition and draw meaning and fulfillment from it. Sometimes, of course, as in the "December 13th" sequence inspired by the legendary figure of Saint Lucy (who remains unnamed), living becomes perilous. In this sequence, the woman is "alive," once "every blow [has been] erased," when she is "beyond all your hands." Yet another key theme informs this sequence associated with Saint Lucy and, in fact, runs throughout *All the Eyes that I Have Opened*: learning how to see, restoring one's sight, gaining new insight. Lucy is the patron saint of the eyes. In paintings, she is often depicted as holding her eyes on a golden plate. Mancinelli evokes this conceit in an image explicitly tracing the passage from wounding and brutal death to an offering: Lucy's "gift" of the eyes so that we can receive from them a vision opening out towards a potentially positive transformation:

> I look at your eyes on the plate
> grains of a vibrating face
> open like the blue
> over a harvested field.

Moreover, Saint Lucy's feast day—a festival of light—precedes Christmas and thus also is an "end" that is simultaneously a "beginning." Before calendar reforms, this feast day took place on the shortest, and therefore darkest, day of the year; after this celebration, more light would gradually come, every day. This book returns often to this theme of seeing and recovering sight. In a text from "Master Trees," for instance, she writes:

> when you see again, you'll find everything supported by branches. Nothing has happened. We're here on this framework of leaves. At times a cry opens the throat. We lose warmth. Then the shaking, cradling us in the light wind.

More often now than previously, Mancinelli has been exploring ancient sources that resonate in the present. A prime example is the sequence "To the tiny bronze offering bearers found on Mount Titano," but there are traces elsewhere in this volume, even in the stark setting of a migrant route in the Balkans. One prose piece from the sequence "Jungle," for example, evokes "a soul among the forks of some branches" that appears to the narrator (a migrant), to whom the poet gives voice. This "soul" is actually a manuscript that has apparently been "kept tightly against [someone's] chest and abandoned after a long journey" in the tree. Passages perhaps transcribed from some old story or sacred text—an "ancient voice"— can be made out on it.

In such ways, Mancinelli writes within an open, undivided conception of time wherein ends and beginnings blend, and the past, the future, and the present intermingle. This is additionally symbolized by the three blank pages that she has intentionally inserted into this book: they signify a recurrent "end and beginning." Speaking, for instance, in the "Mount Titano" sequence to one of the ancient bronze offering bearers, she admits that "in the presence of emptiness / I cannot do anything but ask / to look like you and melt your feet / into lead planting you here / guardian on two legs." The narrative voice is that of poet speaking in the present and asking for something to happen in the future, but it is also that of someone in the remote past who seemingly participates in a votive ritual. Human flesh is symbolically transformed into something sacred, even as Mancinelli seeks to glimpse the means by which we might better acknowledge—recognize—the place of our ephemeral bodies in something vaster, the cosmos taken in its physical but also potential spiritual configurations. A mystical tension can indeed be perceived in her poetry, in which religious dogma is otherwise totally absent. One also senses the importance of "opening," of learning how to open oneself up to something else, to the other, to otherness—to that awaiting form-to-come. This is another lesson that can be learned from a natural element, as from the buzzards in "Diary of Passage" which, perched on tollway fences, "confirm the route. Every now and then they come flying. You recognize them from the strength they draw from the sky. By simply holding their wings open." Mancinelli's emphasis on opening oneself outwards, to metamorphosis, and to transformation indeed hints at thresholds leading beyond the factuality of our existences.

Her gaze beyond the confines and constraints of our social and material world—her resolution to remove walls, boundaries, and other distinctions—is therefore exerted in time, in space, as well as in her depiction of relationships with others. These are oft-amorous situations involving "the other," who is sometimes intensely present in her poems as one who is loved or who was loved (and who has now disappeared from her life). In this respect, the title sequence "All the Eyes that I Have Opened" is emblematic, as she shows, with sometimes harrowing imagery, how "the other," however initially loving and loved, can enter one's existence and cause destruction. In such cases, the poet's creativity stands up to the dismantling of a relationship by pinpointing the destructive phenomena and by accepting the potentially redeeming aspects—the broken-off branch, the newly opened eye—that can help her move forward and "grow" (another recurrent ideal). "I must create so that I will not be destroyed," she has stated. Once again, individual contours blur, blend, are superposed. "I don't believe in partition walls," she writes, "I close my eyes, and go through the image."

As she has progressed from *Mala Kruna*, a "bildungsroman" in verse, through *Mother Dough*, which already extends the autobiographical circumscription of the former collection, and *The Little Book of Passage,* whose acute personal source likewise ramifies into a transformative journey that we all can take, it is clear that *All the Eyes that I Have Opened* shows a still bolder venturing into previously little-explored areas beyond the self. Yet as she crosses previously uncrossed fields, her verse and prose retain all the intensity of her more strictly personal writings. Furthermore, after the verse poetry of *At an Hour's Sleep from Here* and the prose poetry of *The Little Book of Passage,* this new collection combines the two literary forms into a subtly articulated rhythmic structure alternating vision and narration, the former responding to the latter and vice versa. In a strong sense, Mancinelli's effacing of distinctions and blurring of boundaries enables her to continue to be fully present even when the subject matter seems—but only upon a first reading—exclusively oriented towards others. She is fully within the otherness, deeply inside whomever she is not.

This taking into account of other lives and realities is, of course, most vividly exhibited in "Jungle" and "Diary of Passage." Both sequences derive from her participation in the European project "Refest: Images and Words on Refugee Routes." During this project, she traveled, with eight other poets, artists, and photographers, along the itineraries used by migrants on the Balkan Routes. Mancinelli knows all too well that if her poetics of self-transformation—the movement from pain to new possibilities of vision—is well founded, then it must sustain visions of horror and misery. At one point, she in fact wonders why she is there, on the trails: "Perhaps I have obeyed the sound of broken branches, which reaches me from this unknown language, like walking in a dense forest. There is something immediately familiar in these bits of bark that preserve meanings." A tentative answer actually emerges in the next sequence, which is set in another place and alludes to another context. Something—first a sentence in her mind, then a sound, a breath, then breathing—is moving through the poet and asking to take shape, "to have body," a new "place." Already in a train, she is now underway in the deepest, most genuine sense—a kind of inner departure and moving ahead—through writing—that already starts to respond to the question: "Why am I here?"

> how I arrived here, I don't know. Someone asks me for a ticket. I close my eyes. The train keeps gliding, very slowly, through the darkness—I repeat a single sentence become sound, breath. This breathing that moves through me asks to have body. It asks to have a place. Or to go through the space between the eyes, welcomed by the smallest and meekest animals.

Even as the migrants can be broken along the way, and blocked at a border, the poet too has been shattered (by the traumatic experience underlying the sequence "All the Eyes that I Have Opened") and stopped on her life's journey. It is akin to the flow of a river that is "broken up, after a leap or fall" and turns into "foam." A struggle begins "against a moving, impassable boundary," as the prose piece puts it; in other words, a boundary that is also the inner impasse in which one can find oneself after a disaster. But then something can occur and free us, setting us back into the flow of life. By reflecting on the meaning of one's life, of one's being in the encompassing cosmos, and in Mancinelli's case by writing, the liberating movement can commence. The book finishes with these lines:

> I am limpid today, like a windowpane never lined by rain.
> I have forgotten what I have forgotten. I just look. Flocks

fly by. Through the light, warmth is gathered in the woods
on the hill, in my body stretched out at last—I have be-
lieved in the sky. In the broken line of the horizon. Like a
simple outline, a possible form of life.

And yet these same perceptions might equally have been those
of a migrant, a simultaneity underscoring the highly thoughtful
and crafted manner in which the sequences in this book form a
coherent, intricately interrelated whole. The "Diary of Passage"
is their diary of a "step" (as the Italian title "Diario di passo" also
indicates). One could say "the next step," the fundamental change
awaiting them, or her, or us. In this regard, while she has extended
and deepened her psychological, philosophical, and spiritual pur-
view in this new book, she has continued to gather in and preserve,
to protect, what is most helpless and fragile in herself or in others, a
remarkable quality of her earlier work as well. Her poetic language
aspires to bring life—the vital force—to ordinary language, giving
it a transformative energy as well. As she labors over words initially
jotted down in one of her beloved *taccuini*, her "notebooks," she
thereby sets very high standards for herself and for poetic language,
conceiving it in such a way that it will be able to stand up alongside
pain, be it hers or that of others, and be a fitting expression of it, all
the while opening out and pointing ahead.

John Taylor
Saint-Barthélemy d'Anjou
28 February 2023

non può disperdersi
i ricompone a ogni svota
*come uno stormo in **viaggio**.*

cannot scatter itself
puts itself back together at every turn
like a flock flying onwards.

JUNGLE

JUNGLE

quello che posso lo scaldo al fuoco. Abbiamo trovato una pentola di buona fattura. Chi ha bivaccato qui, ora è già forse in Germania. Questione di tempo, di soldi e di fortuna. I soldi li ha presi la nostra guida. Beve energetici da una lattina nera. Ha il sapore di sciroppo per il mio bambino.

※

whatever I can I heat up over the fire. We found a well-made sauce-
pan. Whoever bivouacked here is perhaps already in Germany.
A matter of time, money, and luck. Our guide took the money.
He drinks energy drinks from black cans. It tastes like syrup for
my baby.

meno due gradi oggi. È apparso il sole, un cerchio chiaro come una pietra. Il vestito del mio piccolo steso ad asciugare. Al vento d'acciaio della E70. Muoiono gli animali che escono di notte, per raggiungere l'altra parte del bosco.

Sporca di fango la sua tutina con i cuori –ha piovuto dove abbiamo dormito ieri.– L'ho lasciata su questa recinzione sottile –non c'è tempo per il bucato. Forse domani attraversiamo il confine.

✳

non poteva più parlare ai suoi, né orientarsi con il Gps. –Ieri notte, vicino al fuoco, raccontavano di un ragazzo afghano. Era nel "gioco" da mesi. L'ultima volta era tornato zoppicando sulla scarpa che gli era rimasta. Tremava. Tutta la strada fatta da casa… L'hanno trovato poco lontano da qui. Si è arrampicato su un albero, si è legato a un ramo, e si è lasciato cadere.

✳

two degrees below zero today. The sun appeared, a circle as clear as a stone. The clothes of my little one have been laid out to dry. In the steely wind of the E70 tollway. Animals that come out at night to reach the other part of the forest, die.

His romper suit with hearts is smeared with mud—it rained where we slept yesterday. —I left it on this flimsy fence—there's no time for laundry. Maybe tomorrow we cross the border.

✳

he couldn't speak with his friends and family anymore, nor find his bearings with the GPS. —Last night, near the fire, they were talking about an Afghan boy. He had been in the "game" for months. The last time he had come back limping on his one remaining shoe. He was trembling. All that long road from home. . . They found him not far from here. He had climbed a tree, tied himself to a branch, and let himself drop.

✳

qui non possiamo restare altro tempo. È freddo. Non abbiamo più soldi. Ma possiamo avere fortuna. Prego ogni notte. Stamattina, tra le forcelle dei rami, mi è apparsa un'anima. Corrosa dalla pioggia, si stava lacerando. Stretta al petto di qualcuno e abbandonata dopo un lungo viaggio, ora si apriva al bosco. Una voce antica, raccontava

(…) Gerico.
Era ricco (…) gli chiese (…) non poteva. (…).
Corse avanti (…).

*

we can't stay here any longer. It's cold. We don't have any more money. But we can have luck. Every night I pray. This morning a soul among the forks of some branches appeared to me. Corroded by the rain, it was being lacerated. Kept tightly against someone's chest and abandoned after a long journey, now it was opening itself to the woods. An ancient voice, it was saying

(…) Jericho.
He was rich (…) she asked him (…) he couldn't. (…).
He ran ahead (…).

✳

stringo forte gli occhi non si chiudono. Non riesco a murarmi dentro, a cementare la porta. –Ha già infilato il suo arnese.– Stringo gli occhi. Vedo il nero venato di rosso, le sagome sfumate dei miei avi –lavora di piccone, le mie viscere fatte pietra.– Non è la morte. È soltanto un suo innesto.

Continua a scavare nella fossa deserta. –Altri secondi di nero cupo.

Ora. Cavalo da me. Estrai questo tuo pene marcio.

I close my eyes tight, they won't shut. I can't manage to wall myself up inside, cement the door. —He's already stuck in his tool.— I close my eyes tight. I see blackness veined with red, the hazy shapes of my ancestors —he works with a pickax, my womb turned to stone.— It's not death. It's only one of its grafts.

He keeps digging in the deserted pit. —More seconds of dark blackness.

Now. Pull it out of me. Extract your rotten penis.

dietro questa faccia di cartapesta
risplende in tutti un sorriso perenne.

behind the papier-mâché face
an everlasting smile shines in everyone.

sono le perle del tempo, le morti
le attraversiamo come un filo.

deaths are time's beads
we go through them like a string.

è un chiodo la mattina
trafitta la mente
affiora un'immagine
come da un frutto marcio
torna in piccoli segni
la vita senza forma brulicando.

the morning is a nail
once the mind is pierced
emerges an image
as if from rotten fruit
swarming formless life
comes back in tiny signs.

si è fatta di grafite la pupilla
fissa la nebulosa
di punti che siamo.

turned into graphite the eye
stares at the nebula
of points that we are.

trapassando la terra
nel sonno continuiamo a discendere
in circolo tra organi e pianeti.

passing through the earth
in sleep we keep going down
in circles between organs and planets.

ci svegliamo dentro gli occhi di un uccello.
È questo il mondo, un frutto spezzato
a colazione, il cerchio della tazza
specchio che si apre
su un prato, una coperta
a contenerci come un'isola
da cui non siamo nati.

we awake inside a bird's eyes.
This is the world, fruit sliced
at breakfast, the cup's circle
a mirror that opens out
onto a lawn, a blanket
including us like an island
from which we were not born.

ALBERI MAESTRI

MASTER TREES

ogni giorno per il taglio utile
ricominciare, e mai giungere
a se stessi –spezzata la custodia
della nascita, niente
altro che filamenti buoni al fuoco.

every day for the useful pruning
beginning again and never reaching
oneself —shattered the safekeeping
of birth, nothing
but filaments good for the fire.

fanno un rumore secco
le cose che sono state vive.

things that have been alive
make a sharp crack.

quando tornerai a vedere troverai ogni cosa sorretta dai rami. Non è accaduto niente. Siamo qui, su questa intelaiatura di foglie. A tratti un grido spalanca la gola. Perdiamo tepore. Allora si scuote, ci culla nel vento leggero.

when you see again, you'll find everything supported by branches. Nothing has happened. We're here on this framework of leaves. At times a cry opens the throat. We lose warmth. Then the shaking, cradling us in the light wind.

ho visto gli occhi degli alberi

nel folto una scossa
di chiarore rimasto –a vegliarci
come fitta pioggia che aspetta.

I've seen the eyes of the trees

within the thicket a jolt
of glimmer left —to watch over us
like heavy rain waiting.

ramifico secondo la luce
alberi maestri
a spalancarmi il petto
con la forza che viene da un seme.

I branch out according to the light
master trees
to open my chest wide
with the strength that comes from a seed.

era inerte l'aria, percorsa da tremori e scosse. Bisognava ritrarsi, mettere in serbo la vita, sospingerla verso zone dove si aprivano sacche di quiete. Così sono cresciuto in questa forma amputata. La strada accanto puoi vedere in me come brucia.

the air was inert, traversed by trembling and quivering. It needed to withdraw, to set life aside, to push it towards areas where pockets of quietness opened. I thus grew in this maimed form. You can see in me how the nearby street burns.

non è stato intagliato
non è ancora dentro un viso.
Quando prende parola
la sua presenza trema.

it hasn't been carved
isn't inside a face yet.
When it begins to speak
its presence trembles.

ho iniziato a curvarmi, a prendere la strada del ritorno. Vado incontro ai fratelli che premono –mie biforcazioni notturne.

La superficie si infrange nascendo –la sfioro. Il cielo ha l'odore della mia linfa. Ho circoscritto me stesso. La mia maestosa statura.

I have started to bend, to take the way back. I head towards the brothers who are pushing —my nightly bifurcations.

The surface breaks at birth —I brush against it. The sky has the smell of my sap. I have circumscribed myself. My majestic stature.

dai rami della specie
la nuca, una cima
in ascolto tentenna

tutto l'andare è tornare,
un fascio di legna raccolta.
La sua fiamma mi schiuderà le mani.

from the branches of the species
the nape, a treetop
that listens, hesitates

any going is a going back,
a bundle of gathered wood.
Its flame will open my hands.

da qui partivano vie
respirando crescevo

nel crollo, qualcosa di dolce
un incavo del tempo

tutti gli occhi che ho aperto
sono i rami che ho perso.

from here ways parted
breathing I was growing

in the collapse, something sweet
a hollow of time

all the eyes that I have opened
are the branches that I have lost.

entro nella pioggia come in un bosco
–ali fittamente intessute
aperte e richiuse sotto la scorza.
Cammino, la nuca protetta
dai miei custodi, liberato lo sguardo
dalla gabbia degli occhi.

I go into the rain as into a woods
—wings densely interwoven
opened and closed beneath the bark.
I walk, my nape protected
by my guardians, my gaze freed
from the cage of my eyes.

TUTTI GLI OCCHI CHE HO APERTO

ALL THE EYES THAT I HAVE OPENED

alla polvere dell'aria
ricongiungimi

mia luce che vieni come una miccia.

pietà presto ricopri
il nostro nero andare
tra sonni e gesti.

to the dust of the air
reunite me

my light coming like a fuse.

pity cover over soon
our dark going forward
between sleep and deeds.

una mano muso di serpente
sale la schiena, la carezza
cresce come un'edera sul respiro
di te fa legno secco.

ha i denti questo giorno
come giocando morde
mi incide di sillabe le mani:
tra poco il fiotto affiora.

a hand like a snake's nose
slithers up your back, caresses it
grows like ivy over your breathing
makes dry wood of you.

this day has its teeth
as it plays it bites
lances my hands with syllables:
soon the gush emerges.

non può fare ordine
nelle mie viscere –fruga
alle mie spalle, straripano
i cassetti, rovescia

e ricomincia.

furia di uomo piegato
sulle braccia scuotendomi
–non può aspettare frutti
cadranno pietre
perderò le foglie
al sole arretreranno le mie linfe.

he cannot put my innards
in order, rummages
behind my back —the drawers
are overflowing— overturns them

and begins again.

                              rage of a man bent over
                              his arms shaking me
                              —he cannot wait for fruit
                              stones will fall
                              I'll lose my leaves
                              my saps will withdraw into the sun.

franato dal mondo
il suo corpo di pietra premeva.
–La salvezza era una gabbia d'ossa.

Spezza la chiave
inverte l'ordine di ogni parola
lega la testa ai piedi, in un gorgo
ti chiude gli occhi.

dopo il latte
una manciata di chiodi in bocca

parlare, mangiare
a fondo piantare
una promessa.

rockslide from the world
his stone body pressing down on you.
—Safety was a cage of bones.

He turns and turns the key
inverts the order of every word
ties head to feet, in a whirlpool
closes your eyes.

after the milk
a handful of nails in the mouth

talking, eating
deeply planting
a promise.

tiene un ago tra le labbra
si ricuce masticando
con un filo di lacrime e saliva
punto croce, punto
perché il disegno avanzi, deglutire.

✳

she keeps a needle between her lips
mends while chewing
with a thread of tears and saliva
cross stitch —period
since the pattern progresses
with swallowing.

✳

né pelle né polpa puoi avere
non si ferma la lama, ti conosce
la sua carezza soltanto nel bianco.

il muro della casa è senza porta.
Cosa chiedi, a pugni contro l'aria.
Abbi pace. Neanche fatta formica
trovi una fenditura.

neither skin nor pulp suffice
the blade doesn't stop, its caress
knows you only in what is bone white.

the wall of this house has no door.
Whatever you ask for, fists raised
    against the air.
Be peaceful. Not even as an ant
will you find the slit.

questa faccia è una scarpa.
Contro le pietre si è aperta.

raccogli briciole di vetro
e ciò che cresce dalle crepe,
a ogni centesimo di rame
paziente porgi la ciotola del ventre.

this face is a shoe.
Against the stones it has split open.

you collect bits of glass
and whatever grows from cracks,
to every copper coin
patiently you hold out the bowl
of your belly.

il peso netto del corpo diviso
l'arco di ogni passo è uguale
ai crolli e alle stragi aperte
alla terra ancora
una volta battuta.

Componi la sconfitta
come equazione di un sentiero.

nel mortaio delle mie cavità
per non so quali grani
di finissima polvere
ancora pesti.

the net weight of the divided body
the arc of each footstep is equal
to what collapses and is openly massacred
on the earth once again
trampled on.

Compose the defeat
as the equation of a path.

into the mortar of my body cavities
for who knows what grains
of very fine powder
you keep crushing.

qualcuno dal calcolo
strisciando è sfuggito
–non è mai stato
riconosciuto un corpo.

Nell'intreccio di foglie
stretto ai tronchi succhia la terra.

piantàti tra le tempie
questi bulbi maturano
quando potrai, coprili
nel buio oltre la crosta.

someone from the body count
has crawled away
—never been
recognized as a body.

And among the tangled leaves,
close to the trunks, sucks the soil.

planted between the temples
these bulbs will ripen,
when you can, cover them
in the darkness below the crust.

proiettile nel petto
incastonata gemma
a segnarmi di scie
lentamente trapasserai
il tuo bersaglio nel buio del cosmo.

tagliato il filo
crollano le vertebre.

Finalmente ritorno
tra le tue mani.

bullet in the chest
embedded gem
to mark out trails in me
slowly you will pierce
your target in the cosmic darkness.

when the thread is slashed
the vertebrae collapse.

In the end I return
between your hands.

crescono i capelli ancora, le unghie
il peso è restituito
all'aria. Le mani sono le stesse:
il calore è tornato
del sole. Posso sentire
la tua scossa arrivare
come le foglie dal ramo più alto.

the hair is still growing, so are the nails
the weight is given back
to the air. The hands are the same:
the heat has returned
to the sun. I can feel
your shock arriving
like leaves from the highest branch.

LUMINESCENZE

GLEAMS

dove lo scorrere di un fiume si interrompe, dopo un salto o una cascata, l'acqua torna a farsi schiuma. La corrente così forte da trattenere tutto ciò che giunge. Una lotta inizia contro un confine mobile, invalicabile. –Oscillazioni, brevi tentennamenti. Obbedienza a una lingua bianca e devastante. A volte è un temporale, o un masso contro cui urtare, deviare rotta. E ritrovarsi liberi.

wherever the flow of a river is broken up, after a leap or fall, the water turns back into foam. The current is so strong that it keeps everything that comes. Begins a struggle against a moving, impass-able boundary. —Swaying, brief wavering. Obedience to a white, devastating language. Sometimes it's a storm, or a rock bumped into, deviating the course. And you find yourself free.

corro. E sto fermo all'incrocio
dove rallenta, precipita

per una legge di gioia si trasforma.
Non credo ai muri divisori.
Chiudo gli occhi, e attraverso l'immagine.

I'm running. And standing at the crossroads
where it slows down, falls

is transformed by a law of joy.
I don't believe in partition walls.
I close my eyes, and go through the image.

con la forza del niente
del non avuto mai
niente da barattare,
i gesti ricompongono una lingua
si allaccia al mio corpo un'armatura.

with the power of nothing
of never having had
anything to barter,
gestures re-create a language
fastening armor to my body.

–stanno ancora tessendo,
salda il filo respiro

e accogli tutti i colpi
di un cuore àrmati.

—they're still weaving.
Join up the breath thread

and welcome all the thumps
of a heart you'll arm yourself with.

l'allarme non scatta, ma è un furto
con scasso. L'amore
a tracollo ci porta: sua borsa,
dentro ci mette la nostra miseria.

the alarm doesn't sound yet it's
a break-in. Love's shoulder
strap carries us: its bag,
our neediness stuck inside.

la calpesti ogni giorno
la più piccola grazia,
fiore formica nell'erba che cresce

non ti scordare di me.

every day you tread on
the slightest grace,
an ant-flower in the grass growing

forget me not.

è accaduto, resta: nel cupo
cavo da abitare come un utero

c'è un punto in cui la vita si rovescia
diventa scrittura morse.

it has happened, stay: in the dark
hollow like a uterus, dwell

there is a point when life overturns
becomes Morse code.

al centro il mistero, lo stame
del tempo. Crescono petali
e giorni. Non c'è vaso
né giardino. Soltanto
la terra. La luce. La pioggia.

at the center the mystery, the stamen
of time. Petals grow
and days. There is neither vase
nor garden. Only
the earth. The light. The rain.

＊

nel chiarore d'inizio
curvi sotto una sacca d'amnio
vanno al lavoro, passano –la porta
del sonno si socchiude.

✵

with the first glimmers,
hunched under an amniotic sack
they go to work, pass by —the door
of sleep half opens.

lungo la rete di sangue asfaltato
le ceneri dei luoghi
aspettano di viaggiare
come polvere sacra.

on the asphalt-blood network
the ashes of places
expect to travel
as sacred dust.

ritorno, ascolto l'aria. E poi salto.
I dove sono tutti provvisori.
Crescono come rami.

I come back, listen to the air. And then jump.
The where's are all provisional.
They grow like branches.

punto gli occhi e si compie
la mia area, il cerchio della vita.

I point my eyes and my area
is rounded off, the circle of my life.

negli occhi chiusi una sorgente
di pupille –luminescenze
trascorse tra globi
custodi di un'unica immagine
gravitante nella polvere esplosa.

in closed eyes a wellspring
of pupils —gleams
gone by between globes
guardians of a single image
gravitating in the exploded dust.

l'infinito dei morti
espande un'altra galassia.
Il rosso nel buio continua
a sfociare nel mare
dove siamo senza corpo accucciati.

the infinite dead
expand into another galaxy.
The red within the dark keeps
flowing into the sea
where we crouch bodiless.

il morto si può fare: braccia aperte
per chiglia la colonna, niente
nella mente, un moto
come un ricordo d'acqua.

one can play dead: arms spread,
the backbone for a keel, nothing
in the mind, motion
like a memory of water.

è il giorno, il vento
non si alzerà. Correre
tra fari e bastoni –al molo
pochi metri di lamiera una barca.
Hanno gridato *è grande*
Dio, siamo partiti
a spalle unite, muti
–su ogni nostro respiro
il motore inizia a rompersi in pianto.

the day's come, the wind
won't rise. Running
between beacons and beatings —at the dock
a few meters of sheet-metal boat.
They shouted *great*
is God, we left
shoulder to shoulder, silent
—over our every breath
the engine starts to break into tears.

tutti nella stiva premendo
per un'altra vita l'aria
come una madre manca.
Lotta di gambe e di braccia
–non svuoteranno il mare.
Richiusa in bara la barca discende.

everyone in the hold, pressing
for another life the air
missing like a mother.
Arms and legs wrestling
—they won't empty the sea.
A shut coffin, the boat sinks.

alla deriva, nel moto continuo
anche i gabbiani
passano su di loro senza grida.
Così dopo un incidente
restano sull'asfalto frutti intatti.

adrift, within the constant swell
even the seagulls
fly over them without squawking.
In this way after an accident
they remain intact fruit on the asphalt.

SPECCHIO RICURVO

CURVED MIRROR

è di ossa o di terra
cotta al fuoco la parte
di me in dono, invisibile
occhio che stilla dalla roccia
la grazia. –Quello che è stato
tornerà con la pioggia
affiorando piccoli indizi
e frammenti di un dio.

*

TO THE TINY BRONZE OFFERING BEARERS FOUND ON MOUNT TITANO

it's of bone and earth
baked in fire the part
of me I gift you, invisible
eye that lets grace drip
from the rock. —What has been
will come back with the rain
uncovering minute clues
and fragments of a god.

*

ora inizio a distinguerti,
vieni da un incavo del legno
da forme riconosciute tra i rami
nostri avi ad attenderci –figli
nel cerchio degli anni.

✳

a cospetto del vuoto
non posso fare altro che chiedere
di somigliarti e fonderti –i piedi
nel piombo piantandoti qui
custode su due gambe.

✳

now I begin to make you out,
you come from a hole in wood
from shapes recognized between branches
our ancestors waiting for us —children
in the circle of years.

＊

in the presence of emptiness
I cannot do anything but ask
to look like you and melt your feet
into lead planting you here
guardian on two legs.

＊

una piega, l'inizio di un passo– ti fermi nella luce accecante: non essere. Ma ti hanno scelto. Per la tua innocenza, per il tuo capo rotondo –e quei due piccoli cerchi sul viso. Sarai fuso nel bronzo, ancorato a questa fenditura.

✳

il buio iniziava a disfarsi. Mi sono alzato, ho camminato verso il crinale del monte –potevo attingere a tutta la forza che il giorno disperde attraverso le ore. Saldando la pianta dei piedi, levandomi diritto nella mia statura: la nuca obbediva al chiarore come una corolla.

Quando il sole è sorto, ho mostrato le palme, ho alzato un braccio. Non ho potuto più muovere un passo.

✳

bending forward, the beginning of a footstep— you stop in the blinding light: not to be. But they have chosen you. For your innocence, your round head —and those two tiny circles on your face. You will be cast in bronze, anchored to this thin crack.

❋

the darkness was dissipating. I stood up, walked towards the mountain ridge —I could draw on all the strength that the day disperses hour after hour. Joining the soles of my feet, standing up straight and tall: my nape was obeying the glimmer like the corolla of a flower.

When the sun rose, I held out my palms, I raised an arm. I couldn't take a single step anymore.

❋

ringraziare o chiedere grazia è un solo gesto. Ho aperto le mani. Vi ho trovato una scodella e un cofanetto di incensi. Li reggevo come una bilancia che oscilla, fino a che si è piegato il braccio sinistro, l'altro è risalito a mezz'aria. I piedi erano affondati, congiunti alle fondamenta della terra.

thanking or asking for grace is a single gesture. I opened my hands. There I found a bowl and a box of incense. I held them like a swinging scale until my left arm bent, my other arm rose in midair. My feet had sunk, joined the foundations of the earth.

tutta la forza del mondo
non sposta un raggio di luce

ora sei tu il cardine

–da queste ceneri
ti sto versando la voce

✳

all the world's strength
can't shift a ray of light

now you're the mainstay

—from these ashes
I'm pouring you the voice

✳

io non lascio la terra
io non brucio nel fuoco
come una pietra non posso morire
soltanto aprirmi in una fenditura
dove il pugnale si illumina.

✻

guardo i tuoi occhi sul piatto
grani di un viso che vibra
aperto come l'azzurro
su un campo mietuto.

✻

I'm not leaving the earth
I'm not burning in the fire
like a stone I cannot die
only be opened in a gash
in which your daggers shine

✳

I look at your eyes on the plate
grains of a vibrating face
open like the blue
over a harvested field.

✳

ora che hai ricevuto la palma
dal manto oscuro dell'angelo
stringi la penna non scrive
come un ramo tagliato
altro che l'aria splendente.

✳

specchio ricurvo il dono
riaffiora velato di muschio
ciottolo nella corrente:
cancellato ogni urto, vivo
oltre le vostre mani.

now that you've received the palm
from the angel's dark mantle
clutch the pen it writes nothing
like a cut-off branch
nothing but the shining air.

❋

curved mirror the gift
reemerges veiled in moss
a pebble in the current:
every blow erased, I'm alive
beyond all your hands.

TRE SILLABE DI SILENZIO

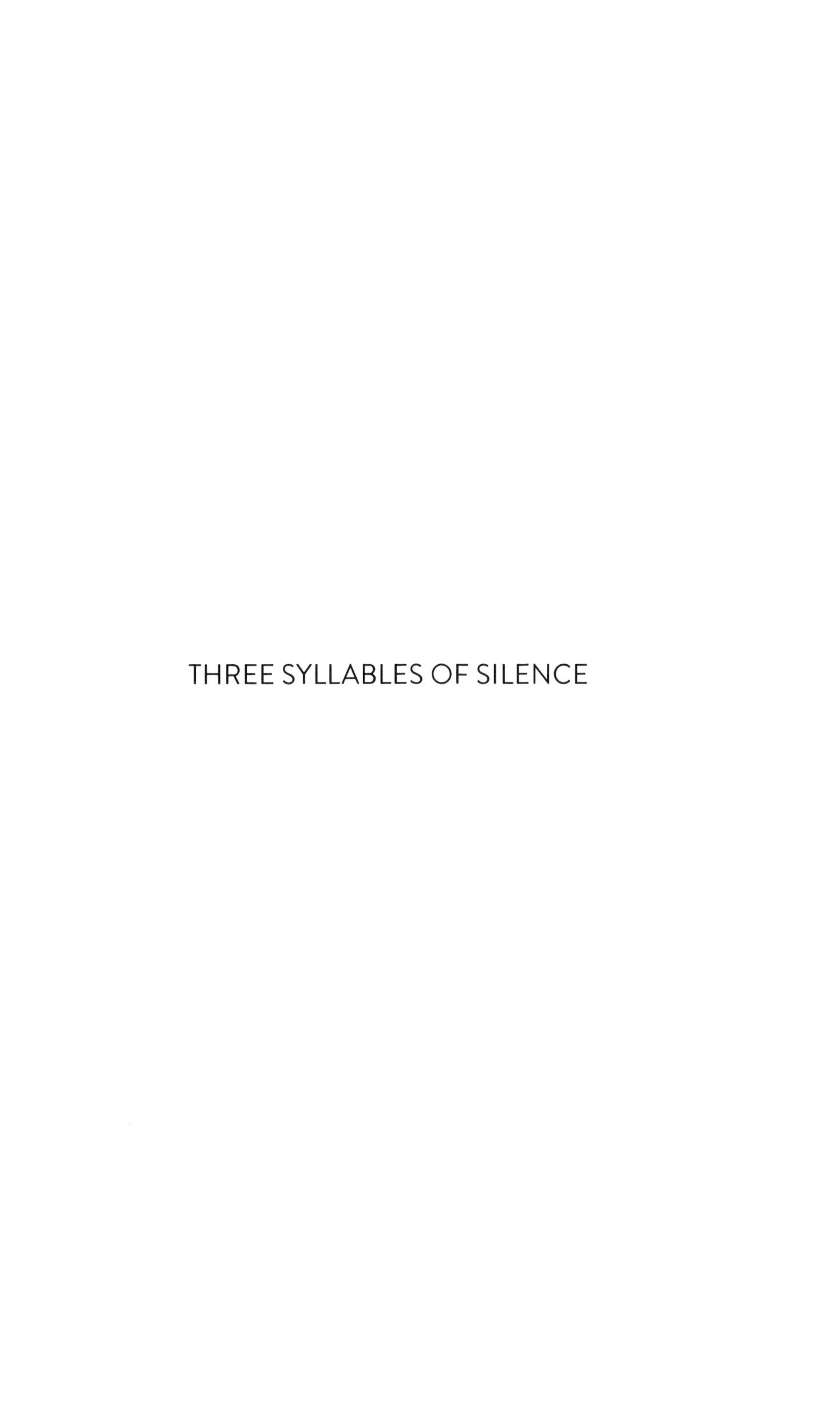

THREE SYLLABLES OF SILENCE

non si chiudono gli occhi.
Vedo da dentro –il buio
dal germe a questo incavo:
scrittura, mia camera oscura.

✳

the eyes don't close.
I see from inside —the darkness
from the seed to this recess:
writing, my darkroom.

✳

aspetto che scenda la luce, resto qui, fino a che iniziano a camminare le pietre. Si schiudono come uova deposte da una madre che si è fatta di sabbia. Affiorano a un tratto le piccole zampe e la testa. Vengono a un mondo che ha già chiuso gli occhi. Mi avvicino: le stringo in una mano, le tengo sul petto. Poi le accompagno a riva, le riconsegno.

I wait for the light to dim, stay here until the stones start walking.
They hatch like eggs laid by a mother who has made herself of sand.
All of a sudden the small legs and the head emerge. They come into
a world that has already closed its eyes. I come closer: I hold them,
place them on my chest. Then I accompany them to the shore, I
hand them back.

nell'errore non mi sbaglio mai.

in erring, I never err.

il dito scatta, trapassa. Il corpo un pianeta disabitato –e l'odore che fa,
tutta la vita in un batterio.

the finger snaps, goes through. The body like an uninhabited planet
—and the smell it makes: an entire life in a bacterium.

a un tavolo di distanza sediamo, ai lati opposti di uno specchio. A tratti affiora una parte del tuo viso o del mio. Ci riconosciamo, socchiudiamo gli occhi. Portiamo qualcosa alla bocca. Con piccoli balzi un passero si allontana e ritorna. Tu hai spezzato il pane. Da uno spazio aperto, da un angolo bianco, aspetti.

Sulla tovaglia un piccolo quadrato premuto dalle tue dita. In una coltivata, operosa distrazione.

we're sitting across a table, on opposite sides of a mirror. Sometimes a part of your face or mine appears. We recognize each other, half-close our eyes. We bring something to our mouths. With little jumps, a sparrow moves off and comes back. You've broken the bread. In an open-ended position, in a blank corner, you are waiting.

On the tablecloth a small square plot pressed down by your fingers. With a cultivated, industrious distraction.

chini la testa da un lato e mi guardi. Hai le braccia aperte, mi porgi un osso. Grande come un femore. Non so se è bianco, se ha ancora un po' di carne.

you bend your head to the side and look at me. Your arms are open, you hand me a bone. As big as a femur. I don't know if it's white, if it still has some flesh.

nelle prime sequenze hai riso e mi hai parlato all'orecchio. Non sapevi di essere dentro l'inquadratura.

✷

da questa distanza posso tenerti a fuoco. Ferma, come negli attimi prima. Le tue ceneri portate dal vento, nella mia camera oscura.

in the first sequences, you laughed and talked into my ear. You didn't know you were inside the framing of the photo.

✳

at this distance I can keep you in focus. You stand still, as in the first moments. Your ashes carried by the wind, into my darkroom.

✳

stringe la stanza come una mano
due pezzi di pane a sbriciolarsi

corpo e sangue di nessuno
fate questo dimenticando
di voi solo un residuo
da spazzare via.

✷

the room squeezes like a hand
crumbling two bits of bread

body and blood of no one
do this in forgetfulness
of yourselves mere remains
to be swept away.

in me ora scrivi con inchiostro bianco
di questo nulla portato a compiersi:

queste pagine di cartilagine
sono lo scheletro dove ti aggiri
come un'ombra nel sangue.

in me now you write in white ink
of this nothing brought to completion:

these cartilage pages
are the skeleton in which you roam
like a shadow of blood.

oggi è sorto dalle mie acque.
A palme sul ventre, cresce
raggiunge il centro, risplende.
Mi alzo e si moltiplica –il corpo
è una giostra di minime ali.

non cresce, non mette radici.
Quello che porti è reciso.
Ho acqua tiepida e buia
nel mio vaso di carne
per farlo vivere.

today has emerged from my waters.
With my palms on my womb, it grows
reaches the center, shines.
I get up and it multiplies —the body
is a merry-go-round of minute wings.

doesn't grow, doesn't take root.
What you bring is snipped off.
I have dark lukewarm water
in my vase of flesh
to keep it alive.

vede dal corpo
come da bocca aperta.
È un rabdomante di precipizi.
Negli occhi ha schegge di ossidiana.

in ruminare paziente
ti sta divorando la vita, sazio
come una carestia.

he sees from the body
as from a gaping mouth.
He can divine precipices.
Obsidian chips are in his eyes.

patiently ruminating
he's devouring your life, he's full
like a famine.

siamo noi, polline e polvere.
Poche ore per ere di lontananza.
Come la chioma di un albero prima
della bufera. Avere due occhi
riconoscerti. Di ogni tuo nome
porto alla bocca
tre sillabe di silenzio.

that's us, pollen and dust.
A few hours for eras of distance.
Like the crown of a tree before
the storm. Having two eyes,
recognizing you.
Of every name you've had
I bring to my mouth
three syllables of silence.

FRAMMENTI PER UNA DEDICA

FRAGMENTS FOR A DEDICATION

la visione infrange la superficie della realtà come un sasso uno specchio d'acqua. Correnti e stili si succedono. La superficie del reale si incrina e ricompone. Questo cerchio in cui ci troviamo, sottile e prossimo a svanire, vive nelle vibrazioni di una mano che preme la parete di una caverna.

the vision shatters the surface of reality as would a stone, water. Currents and styles follow each other. The surface of reality breaks and is put back together. This thin, nearly vanishing circle in which we find ourselves lives in the vibrations of a hand pressing against the wall of a cave.

|

il ritratto di chi
si china come pregando a uno specchio:
la luce è la lingua di un luogo.

✳

|

the portrait of one who
bends down as if praying to a mirror:
light is the language of a place.

※

gattonare oltre nell'immenso
della stanza, seguire una storia
di losanghe. Ma dove
il muro finisce, una fiumana
di luce abbaglia. Resto
nel battesimo di questa finestra.

✳

e girano sopra di me le stelle,
api intorno alla mia polvere d'oro

scendono facce
mi insegnano a ridere –io
apro e chiudo gli occhi nella culla.

✳

crawling beyond the immensity
of the room, following a story
of diamond shapes. But where
the wall ends, a flood
of light dazzles. I remain
in the baptism of this window.

❋

and above me revolve the stars,
bees around my golden dust

faces come down
teach me to laugh —I open
and close my eyes in the cradle.

❋

non più lacrime o
confini sigillati da una fiamma

tutti lentamente smettere
come la pioggia che ridona all'aria,
a un tratto come le stelle
di luce spegnerci insieme.

✳

dai talloni alle tempie
si allunga dentro me
come l'ombra di un dio.

no more tears or
confines sealed by a flame

everyone stops slowly
like rain returning to the air,
suddenly like the stars
our lights we snuff together.

＊

from heel to forehead
it lengthens inside me
like the shadow of a god.

II

dipingo a occhi chiusi la finestra
come una tela vuota
tastando i petali appassiti
per prendere colore
–in un vaso i compagni
che aspetto dall'inverno.

✳

ci sono intere colline di occhi
spalancati alla luce,
per non impazzire li ho colti
e guardati in un vaso
–mentre ti aspetto, più denso
si fa nel giallo l'impasto di morte.

II

eyes closed, I paint the window
like an empty canvas,
touching the withered petals
to take their color
—in a vase the company
I expect from winter.

✳

whole hills filled with eyes
staring at the light,
to keep from going mad I've picked
and watched them in a vase
—while I wait for you, death's impasto
grows denser in yellow.

sepoltura. E inizio.
Sono invasata. Vivo in custodia
della terra, a mani immerse
come radici lavorando.

✳

sulle pareti le ferite
sono affiorate dentro una cornice
come un'opera della vita.

III

burial. And beginning. I am potted
and possessed. I live in the earth's
safekeeping, with hands sunk
like roots at work.

the wounds on the walls
have surfaced inside a frame
as a work of life.

la terra, una pagina scura:
ciò che cade si scrive
frantuma e sgrana
nel buio raggiunge
il senso, si perde.

earth, an obscure page:
what happens is written
shatters and crumbles
in the darkness reaches
meaning, is lost.

il mare cambia la terra
si muove per scie di arature
correnti di semine, strade
che affondano. Piccole luci
lontano le case si fanno candele:
ché la notte pronunci
ogni gesto del giorno.

the sea changes the earth
moves through furrows,
rows of sowing, roads
that sink. Tiny lights
faraway the houses turn into candles:
so the night can pronounce
the day's every deed.

ogni città è una radura
–terra battuta per dormire,
polvere e braci spente.

every city is a clearing
—beaten earth for sleeping,
dust and burnt-out embers.

DIARIO DI PASSO

DIARY OF PASSAGE

non è un caso che sia caduta la neve, coprendo questa terra, cancellando le tracce di tutti quelli che hanno vegliato e bivaccato al confine, portati da treni e ore di cammino, con uno zaino, una borsa, sorvegliati dalla polizia e dalle forze speciali schierate come un'altra rete di filo spinato. La neve è caduta su tutto questo, ha ristabilito la pace che ora calpestiamo: questo silenzio, questa solitudine di alberi carichi dei frutti del gelo.

it's no coincidence that snow has fallen, covering this land, erasing the traces of all those who have stayed awake and bivouacked at the border, after riding on trains and walking for hours with a backpack, a bag, watched by the police and special forces deployed like another barbed wire net. The snow has fallen on all this, restoring the peace that we now trample: this silence, this solitude of trees laden with frosty fruit.

✳

Era una valle divisa da un corso d'acqua, dove i bambini si tuffano, appendendosi ai rami, e sulle rive gli adulti li aspettano con il barbecue. C'erano feste da una sponda all'altra, d'estate, nei paesi, e molti amori.

Poi sono affiorate le spine. Chilometri di spirali avvolte su se stesse. Si è srotolato un nastro bianco e rosso, come un segnale di pericolo. Ci siamo recintati –racconta un abitante di Kraj Donji.– Gli animali non lo capiscono. Per questo ogni tanto troviamo un cervo dissanguato. È come un sacrificio che si ripete.

✻

Il confine di Kraj Donji sembra vuoto. Una piccola stazione di guardia deserta. Nell'aria sotto zero una bandiera a strisce rossa, bianca, blu. A pochi passi di distanza, oltre il manto di neve intatto, un'altra piccola stazione e una bandiera con gli stessi colori, in un ordine diverso: bianco, blu, rosso. Al centro questo spazio da cui si resta a guardare, sporti su un precipizio invisibile. A un tratto, dietro una parete di ghiaccio, domanderanno una carta che attesti chi sei.

Ripeto la stessa domanda al viso che appare in una tessera tra lettere e numeri. A questa operazione manca una cifra per essere compiuta. Riempi la tua casella di morte.

✻

It was a valley divided by a stream where children hanging from the branches would dive in and adults await them with a barbecue. In summer, there were parties from one bank to the other, in the villages, and many loves.

Then the thorns emerged. Miles of spirals wrapped around themselves. A red-and-white ribbon was unrolled as a danger sign. We are fenced off —says an inhabitant of Kraj Donji.— Animals don't understand. This is why we occasionally find a deer bled to death. It is like a recurrent sacrifice.

❋

The Kraj Donji border seems vacant. A small deserted guard station. In the below-zero air, a red, white and blue striped flag. A few steps away, beyond the intact mantle of snow, another small station and a flag with the same colors in a different order: white, blue, red. At the center, this space in which one stands, watching, leaning on an invisible cliff. Suddenly, behind an icy wall, they will ask for a card proving who you are.

I repeat the same question to the face that appears on a card between letters and numbers. One figure is missing for this operation to be completed. Fill in your death box.

❋

Non puoi perdere o dimenticare in questo viaggio. La carta che devi conservare nel gioco, e continuare a mostrare, per ribadire che sei della squadra di chi può andare avanti, di chi ha tutto in regola. Che sia con te sempre. Stretta nel tuo portafogli. Cucita a doppio filo alla pelle.

✳

Se a questa dogana solitaria, che taglia in due un piccolo paese nella neve, sovrapponi un fotogramma di un'altra sequenza di tempo (autunno 2015), vedi migliaia di migranti attendere in piedi, sotto la pioggia, o appoggiati a terra l'uno sull'altro. Come si è composta questa immagine? Com'è svanita?

✳

You cannot lose or forget on this journey. The card that you have to keep in the game and keep showing to reiterate you are a member of the team of those who can go on, who have everything in order. May it always be with you. Tight in your wallet. Double-stitched to your skin.

✳

If this solitary customs post, which cuts in two a small village in the snow, is superposed on a snapshot from another sequence of time (autumn 2015), you see thousands of migrants standing and waiting in the rain, or leaning against each other on the ground. How was this image put together? How has it vanished?

✳

Didascalie di sequenze cancellate, le parole di un volontario incontrato a Zagabria.– Sono venuto in treno con loro. Mi hanno scambiato per afghano, per la barba forse e i capelli scuri. Seduti nei corridoi, le gambe e le braccia intrecciate, un'impalcatura umana che oscillava e tremava ai sobbalzi del viaggio. Cantavo con loro, inni nazionali e antiche canzoni. Ripetevo le sillabe, come un bambino, seguendo il suono.

Scesi dal treno, un unico grande branco si muoveva: a destra, a sinistra, *salire sull'autobus*. Erano le tartarughe a dirigerlo. Protette nel loro guscio, sorvegliavano ogni passaggio. Siamo arrivati a Bregana. Il doppio degli abitanti di questa manciata di case. Dai biancheria pulita a una donna e vedi altre venti persone che restano senza. Qualsiasi cosa fai, si scioglie come un fiocco di neve sulle mani.

✳

Captions of deleted sequences, the words of a volunteer met in Zagreb.— I came by train with them. They mistook me for an Afghan, because of my beard maybe and dark hair. Seated in the corridors, arms and legs entangled, a human scaffolding wavering and trembling with the jolts of the journey. I sang with them, national anthems and old songs. Like a child, I repeated the syllables, following the sound.

Once out of the train, a single large crowd was moving: to the right, to the left, *to get on the bus*. The crowd was directed by the turtles. Protected inside their shells, they watched over every passage. We arrived in Bregana. Two times as many of us as the inhabitants of this handful of houses. You give a woman clean laundry and see twenty other people who are left without any. Whatever you do, it melts like a snowflake on your hands.

✳

Casette di legno immerse nel bianco, si guardano da una riva e l'altra di un piccolo corso d'acqua. La recinzione di filo spinato si confonde con quella di orti e giardini privati. Il paese è stato tagliato a metà. Per raggiungere i vicini di fronte, il percorso si è fatto più scomodo e lungo. Nell'ultima casa prima del ponte, una bandierina croata pende da una catasta di legna. A poca distanza ricomincia il bosco, qualche abete maestoso e poi il fitto di rami. Tra gli alberi e le case lo stesso silenzio. Soltanto un anziano oltrepassa l'uscio, zoppicando, inizia lentamente a spalare.

Little wooden houses immersed in the whiteness look at each other from one bank to the other of a small stream. The barbed wire fence merges with those of vegetable patches and private gardens. The village has been cut in half. To reach the neighbors on the other side, the path has become longer and more uncomfortable. In the last house before the bridge, a Croatian flag hangs from a woodpile. A short distance away, the forest begins again, a few majestic firs and then the tangle of branches. The same silence between the trees and the houses. Only one old man comes out of his house, limping, slowly starting to shovel.

non so perché sono qui. Forse ho obbedito al suono di rami spezzati, che mi raggiunge da questa lingua sconosciuta, come camminando dentro l'intrico di un bosco. C'è qualcosa di immediatamente familiare in queste scorze che custodiscono un significato. Basta ripetere il nome di un luogo come Zagreb o Kraj Donji, perché qualcosa di misterioso si muova, come raggi che bucano il fitto dei rami, o la scia di un animale transitato nel folto. È l'incanto di un mondo preverbale, di spiriti buoni e maligni, che immediatamente mi avvolge e risucchia a sé, oltre la soglia in cui si può compiere una decisione, formulare una scelta.

Questa terra è per me l'altra riva del mare. In certe mattine più nitide, dai primi contrafforti dell'Appennino o da uno degli alti colli sulla costa marchigiana, puoi vederla affiorare come una nuvola all'orizzonte. E invece è proprio una terra che ricomincia, dopo le prime miglia marine e i segni delle nasse, oltre le stazioni sospese delle piattaforme, e l'acqua che si fa più profonda e blu, precipitando verso una bellezza che si moltiplica in piccole isole. Se parti in barca a vela la notte dal porto di Pesaro, all'alba ti accoglie il faro di Susak. Basta pronunciare il suo nome, riconoscerlo sulla mappa, per sentire con certezza l'inizio di un altro mondo. O guidare sulla panoramica del Monte San Bartolo: tra una curva e l'altra, a tratti affiora dalla radio questa lingua frammentata e oscura come ciò che viene dall'altro lato di uno specchio.

Ma a venirti incontro, questa volta, è una terra gelata di confini taglienti e di piccole case richiuse in se stesse. Come se la lente dell'inverno restituisse l'immagine nitida, ricongiunta alla sua essenza. È

I don't know why I'm here. Perhaps I have obeyed the sound of broken branches, which reaches me from this unknown language, like walking in a dense forest. There is something immediately familiar in these bits of bark that preserve meanings. It suffices to repeat the name of a place like Zagreb or Kraj Donji to make something mysterious move, like sunrays penetrating entwined branches, or the trail of an animal through a thicket. It is the enchantment of a preverbal world, of good and evil spirits, which immediately envelops me and swallows me back into it, beyond the threshold where a decision can be made, a choice formulated.

For me, this land is the other seashore. On some clearer mornings, from the first foothills of the Apennines or from one of the high slopes on the Marche coast, you can see it emerge like a cloud on the horizon. And nonetheless, it is a land that starts again, after the first nautical miles and the signs of the fish pots, beyond the suspended oil platforms, and the water that becomes deeper and blue, plummeting towards a beauty multiplied by small islands. If you leave on a sailboat at night from the port of Pesaro, at dawn you are greeted by the lighthouse of Susak. It suffices to say its name, recognize it on the map, to definitely feel the beginning of another world. Or drive on the panoramic road of Monte San Bartolo: between one curve and another, at times this fragmented and obscure language emerges from the radio like something coming from the other side of a mirror.

But coming to meet you, this time, is a land frozen with sharp boundaries and small houses shut up into themselves. As if the

sempre questo che cerco, oltre il germoglio e la chioma, il disegno nudo, la trama dei rami come nervature della vita. Soltanto allora appaiono, tra le forcelle, le sagome scure dei nidi abbandonati e le sfere del vischio. A volte si fermano le cornacchie o i grandi corvi neri, in stormi che riempiono i rami come frutti. Basta un segnale invisibile, qualcosa che transita nell'aria, perché l'albero torni consegnato a se stesso. Questa è la cosa più importante accaduta in viaggio attraverso la Slavonia innevata, nel silenzio interrotto dallo scatto, appena percettibile, di una lente che si apre e richiude. Sono le palpebre dei miei compagni che cercano di catturare la realtà. Mentre io guardo e segno sul taccuino qualcosa che assomiglia alle impronte di uccelli sulla neve. Non sarò in grado di leggerle, ma le lascio comunque, fidando in qualcuno che è in transito dentro di me, un cacciatore in cammino su questa pista. Quando io sarò lontana e lui sarà qui, in queste parole si compirà la forma di ciò che sta accadendo.

I corvi sono venuti per lasciarti un insegnamento. Il più difficile. Quei frutti neri sui rami, quella presenza inattesa. E a un tratto il distacco, il vuoto che ritorna limpido. Lo chiami *abbandono*, prova a riconoscerlo come *restituzione*.

✳

Il mio corpo ha una trama aperta da cui pende un filo. Qualcuno all'altro capo, senza neanche accorgersi lo tende, e io lentamente mi assottiglio. Vengo richiamata dall'assenza. Mi avvicino agli spiriti del freddo, a quel nucleo bianco, senza parola, che governa questa terra. Chiudo gli occhi, come pervasa da un mare piatto, senza colore.

✳

lens of winter had returned the clear-cut image, reunited with its essence. This is what I always seek: beyond the bud and the foliage, the nude drawing; branches woven together like nerves of life. Only then do the dark shapes of abandoned nests and the spheres of mistletoe appear between the forks of trees. Sometimes crows or large black ravens make a halt, in flocks that fill the branches like fruit. An invisible signal suffices, something goes by in the air, so that the tree is handed back to itself. This is the most important thing that happened during the trip through snow-covered Slavonia, in the silence interrupted by the barely audible clicks of lenses that open and close. They are the eyelids of my companions who are trying to capture reality. While I watch and, in my notebook, mark something that looks like bird tracks on the snow. I will not be able to read them, but I leave them anyway, trusting someone who is in transit inside me, a hunter walking on this trail. When I am far away and he is here, the form of what is happening will be fulfilled in these words.

The ravens have come to leave you with a lesson. The most difficult one. Those black fruits on the branches, that unexpected presence. And suddenly the detachment, the emptiness that comes back clearly. You call it *abandonment*, try to recognize it as a *restitution*.

✳

My body has an open texture from which hangs a thread. Someone at the other end, without even noticing, pulls it, and slowly I grow thin. The absence beckons me. I approach the spirits of the cold, that white wordless nucleus which governs this earth. I close my eyes, as if pervaded by a flat colorless sea.

✳

Sto iniziando a tradurre la neve. È l'esperienza del deserto. Puoi sentirlo avanzare lentamente, con i suoi granelli gelidi, fino a entrarti nel respiro. Per quanto arretri cercando rifugio in te stessa, nel tuo nucleo di calore sepolto, troverai un seme di ghiaccio. Devi arginarlo con tutte le forze.

Forse ora comprendi i suoni duri di questa lingua che ti ha richiamata e i gesti stranieri in cui hai cercato casa, come in un fitto cespuglio di spine.

❋

Le poiane ci sorvegliano. Appollaiate sui reticolati dell'autostrada, confermano la rotta. Ogni tanto vengono in volo. Le riconosci dalla forza che attingono dal cielo. Tenendo semplicemente le ali aperte.

❋

Dalla pianura innevata mi vengono incontro gli alberi. Soli e se stessi, conoscono il segreto per resistere in questo paesaggio. Una volta sono apparsi come un'oasi. Lo sguardo poteva attingere a quelle sagome scure e nutrirsi, dopo sequenze che si allungano e sfumano a pochi passi dal nulla.

Questo deserto non assomiglia a quello di cui parla Jabès. Puoi perderti nella sua desolazione fino allo sfinimento, e ritrovarti di fronte la durezza di porte chiuse e di confini marcati. Una legge eseguita come un gioco implacabile. Lo straniero, «l'inviato di Dio», deve avere con sé tutte le carte che certificano la sua provenienza celeste.

❋

I'm starting to translate snow. It is the experience of the desert. You can feel it slowly advancing, with its icy grains, until it gets into your breathing. As long as you withdraw, seeking refuge in yourself, in your core of buried heat, you will find a seed of ice. You must contain it with all your strength.

Perhaps now you understand the harsh sounds of this language that has beckoned you and the foreign gestures in which you have sought a home, as in a thick thorny bush.

✳

The buzzards watch over us. Perched on the tollway fences, they confirm the route. Every now and then they come flying. You recognize them from the strength they draw from the sky. By simply holding their wings open.

✳

From the snowy plain, trees come toward me. Alone and just themselves, they know the secret of resisting in this landscape. Once, they appeared as an oasis. By looking, one could draw on those dark shapes and nourish oneself, after sequences of images that extend and fade away a few steps from nothingness.

This desert does not resemble the one of which Jabès speaks. You can lose yourself in its desolation until you become exhausted and find yourself facing the harshness of closed doors and marked boundaries. A law executed as a relentless game. The foreigner, "God's envoy," must have with him all the papers attesting to his heavenly origin.

✳

Ultimo lembo di Slavonia. Gli alberi sono fulmini scuri conficcati nella pianura. Attraversiamo lentamente la *no man's land* che si apre tra Croazia e Serbia. Tra un casello e l'altro dell'autostrada, tra una dogana e l'altra, quest'ampia fascia di spazio si può riconoscere come un'area di sosta, mentre molto altro trascorre ai margini dello sguardo senza trovare parola.

Stiamo entrando in un altro alfabeto. Il manto stradale si fa dissestato. I segnali illeggibili. Ferme sullo steccato ai margini dell'autostrada, le poiane continuano a confermare la rotta. O a sorvegliare un confine in cui non siamo ammessi.

Sulla strada parallela, in direzione opposta, la lunga coda di camion è ferma. Queste lamiere possono nascondere uomini. Ogni tanto vengono scoperti, maltrattati dalla polizia, e ricacciati indietro.

✳

Adaševci. Entriamo nell'autogrill, come nella sosta di una qualsiasi gita, stiamo per prendere un caffè, quando una voce dice: *non ne avrete bisogno*. E siamo subito fuori. Ognuno consegnato a se stesso.

In qualsiasi direzione muova i tuoi prossimi passi, si aprirà un sentiero sottile come un filo, risucchiato dal tuo passo seguente. Il sentiero è in questo spazio che si apre e richiude. Come una cucitura invisibile. Un edificio e la sua cancellata. Una lunga stanza piena di letti a castello. *Entrance* dichiara un cartello sulla porta a vetri. La stessa parola trascritta nell'alfabeto arabo e cirillico. Al cancello ripetono che non è possibile entrare, due sorveglianti in divisa blu, con il cerchio di stelle dell'Europa sulla schiena. Per tutto il tempo, cammina avanti e indietro, con un cellulare all'orecchio, un uomo

The last edge of Slavonia. The trees are dark lightning bolts driven into the plain. We slowly cross the no-man's-land that opens out between Croatia and Serbia. Between one tollway booth and the other one, between one customs post and the other one, this wide strip of space can be recognized as a rest area, while much more happens on the margins of one's gaze without finding a word.

We are entering another alphabet. The road surface becomes uneven. The signs are illegible. Sitting on the fence along the edges of the tollway, the buzzards continue to confirm the route. Or to watch over a border where we are not allowed.

On the parallel road, in the opposite direction, the long line of trucks is at a standstill. The plates of sheet metal can hide men. Occasionally they are discovered, ill-treated by the police, and pushed back.

✳

Adaševci. As on any trip, we enter the rest stop to take a break, are about to have a coffee when a voice says: *you won't need it.* And suddenly we're outside. Each of us left to himself.

In whatever direction your next steps move, a path as thin as a thread will be opened, swallowed up by your next step. The path is within this space that opens and closes back up. Like an invisible seam. A building and its rail fence. A long room full of bunk beds. *Entrance* declares a sign on the glass door. The same word transcribed in the Arabic and Cyrillic alphabets. At the gate, two watchmen in blue uniforms, with the circle of European stars on their backs, repeat that it is not possible to enter. All the while, a man with a coat and thongs walks up and down, with a cell phone

con cappotto e infradito. –Non arriva il suono della sua voce, diretta a un paese lontano.– Uno stormo di passeri viene a posarsi sulla ringhiera. Compone per qualche minuto il proprio messaggio. E in un battito lo fa scomparire rientrando nel fitto del bosco.

✳

Un paio di pantaloni blu e un asciugamano verde sono appesi all'alta recinzione che circonda il campo di Adaševci. Tornerà qualcuno a riprenderseli. Altrimenti appartengono al bosco, all'intrico di tronchi che si contorcono nel gelo. Crescono nel fango cosparso di foglie scure e di una strana precoce fioritura, ultimi residui di neve sporca. È un manto intessuto di detriti, il lascito di esistenze che hanno dimorato qui e poi sono state sradicate e trascinate altrove.

Raggiungo un grande copertone di gomma da cui si diramano due sentieri. Dal fitto dei rami compaiono capanne di legni legati a brani di incerata. Mi fermo ad ascoltare i fantasmi dei camion che passano.

Perché sei qui? Scrivo e il freddo mi paralizza le mani. Sono sulla soglia di una capanna vuota: un focolare di mattoni, una pentola nera. Bucce di cipolla sparse, una lattina di una bevanda energetica. Tra gli alberi si alza un filo di fumo. Dalla capanna più lontana, due sagome accovacciate stanno facendo vento con un cartone. Sto per avanzare quando qualcosa mi richiama indietro, verso il sentiero di terra battuta che corre ai margini del bosco, costeggiando la E70 fino al confine. Una rete sottile lo protegge dalla strada. Lì è appesa una tutina gialla, sporca di terra, con disegnati cuori ed elefanti.

on his ear. —The sound of his voice, directed to a distant country, cannot be heard.— A flock of sparrows alights on the railing. They compose their own message for a few minutes. And with a beating of wings, they make it disappear by returning to the thick of the forest.

✳

A pair of blue pants and a green towel hang from the high fence surrounding Adaševci Camp. Someone will come back to retrieve them. Otherwise they belong to the woods, to the entangled tree trunks, writhing in the frost, which grow in the mud strewn with dark leaves and a strange early flowering or the last remnants of dirty snow. It is a mantle interwoven with debris, the legacy of existences that have dwelled here and then been uprooted and dragged elsewhere.

I reach a large rubber tire from which two paths branch off. From the thicket of branches appear huts of wood tied to pieces of tarp. I stop to listen to the ghosts of passing trucks.

Why are you here? I write and the cold paralyzes my hands. I am on the threshold of an empty hut: a brick hearth, a black pot. Scattered onionskins, an energy-drink can. A wisp of smoke rises between the trees. From the farthest hut, two crouching shapes are making wind with a piece of cardboard. I'm about to move forward when something calls me back towards the dirt path that runs along the edge of the forest, along the E70 tollway to the border. Flimsy net fencing protects it from the road. A yellow jumpsuit soiled with dirt, with heart and elephant designs, is hanging there.

come sono arrivata qui, non lo so. Qualcuno mi chiede un biglietto. Chiudo gli occhi. Il treno continua a scorrere, lentissimo, attraverso il buio –ripeto una sola frase– fatta suono, soffio. Questo respiro che mi attraversa chiede di avere corpo. Chiede di avere luogo. O transitare nello spazio tra gli occhi, intercettato dai più piccoli e buoni animali.

how I arrived here, I don't know. Someone asks me for a ticket. I close my eyes. The train keeps gliding, very slowly, through the darkness —I repeat a single sentence— become sound, breath. This breathing that moves through me asks to have body. It asks to have a place. Or to go through the space between the eyes, welcomed by the smallest and meekest animals.

un gesto può cadermi di mano e rompersi. Allora mi fermo in ginocchio. Chiamo ogni frammento, anche quelli diventati polvere. Nella mia mano vuota, aperta.

a gesture can fall from my hand and break. Then I kneel down. I call out to every fragment, even those that have become powder. In my empty, open hand.

l'albero incandescente. Ha aperto i rami nel tremore. L'anima ful-
minata. Tra queste pareti di pelle e di vene, affiora l'azzurro, come
da un tessuto logoro.

Riconoscere, ricordare la mano. Ruotare lentamente, togliermi
via da qui.

the glowing tree. It has opened the branches within the tremor. The lightning-struck soul. Between these walls of skin and veins, the blue emerges as if from a threadbare fabric.

Recognizing, remembering the hand. Rotating slowly, taking myself away from here.

aspetto che sorga il caffè dalla corolla. Un pulsante, il fiore azzurro svanisce. Non bevo. Apro la finestra: l'aria è fresca, ferma, come dentro al frigo. Un mondo ordinato. Richiudo. Ho in bocca il tempo, i suoi granelli di zucchero. Un regalo, da bambina, stretto tra due dita. Ora cerco la pace di un bicchiere d'acqua –di montagna, un piccolo lago. Svuotato in una cascata. Mi hanno detto che la pillola va ingoiata senza mordere. Intera.

I wait for the coffee to surge from the corolla. A button and the blue flower vanishes. I do not drink. I open the window: the air is fresh, still, as in the fridge. An ordered world. I close the window. I have time in my mouth, its grains of sugar. A gift, as a child, held between two fingers. Now I look for the peace of a glass of water —from the mountains, a small lake. Emptied into a waterfall. They told me that the pill should be swallowed without biting. Whole.

sono limpida oggi, come un vetro mai rigato dalla pioggia. Ho dimenticato cosa ho dimenticato. Guardo soltanto. Gli stormi passano. Attraverso la luce si raccoglie il tepore nel bosco sulla collina, nel mio corpo finalmente disteso –ho creduto al cielo. Alla linea spezzata dell'orizzonte. Come una sagoma semplice, una possibile forma di vita.

I am limpid today, like a windowpane never lined by rain. I have forgotten what I have forgotten. I just look. Flocks fly by. Through the light, warmth is gathered in the woods on the hill, in my body stretched out at last —I have believed in the sky. In the broken line of the horizon. Like a simple outline, a possible form of life.

Notes and Acknowledgments

This book contains three sets of blank pages, an end and a beginning that is repeated.

✴

The sequence *Jungle* is set in the woods near Adaševci (Serbia), on the border with Croatia. With the closing of the Croatian border (in March 2016), the refugees on the "Balkan Route" have found themselves trapped between a hostile bureaucracy and risky illegal itineraries. "Jungle" is what the refugees call the wooded areas where they camp out while waiting to cross the border. If discovered, they are pushed back by the police, through violence and humiliation. This is the "game" that is repeated several times, despite the detailed reports of the NGOs. The "soul among the forks of some branches" is an Arabic manuscript abandoned in the woods near the refugee camp of Adaševci. The manuscript was found by the Bosnian photographer Mitar Simikić. Thanks to his photograph and to Marway Fawzi's help, a few fragments have been translated.

The poems "the morning is a nail" and "turned into graphite the eye" accompanied drawings by Juan Carlos Ceci for his installation "Il peso dell'ombra" ("The Weight of Shadow") at the 2018 Drawing Biennial in Rimini, Italy.

The sequence *Master Trees* resulted from a collaborative project, involving poetry and drawing, with the artist Sebastiano Guerrera.

To the tiny bronze offering bearers found on Mount Titano. These bronze figurines, along with some coins and ceramic votive offerings, are the main vestiges of an ancient place of worship, located on a small plateau of Mount Titano (San Marino) and going back the end of the 5th century B.C. A strip of lead, which was melted, allowed the statuettes to remain embedded in cracks in the rock. The poet's artist-friend Juan Carlos Ceci discovered these bronze figurines in the 1980s and accompanied her to the site for a project that he curated for the Department of Human Sciences at the University of San Marino.

The sequence *December 13th* derives from the images of Saint Lucy's life, through various paintings devoted to her, in particular Lorenzo Lotto's "Saint Lucy before the Judge" (Jesi, Pinacoteca civica).

Fragments for a Dedication. The poems of the first sequence comprise a few images and lines of verse taken from the poetry of Franco Loi. The poems were published in the special issue, of the review *Cenobio* (October-December 2019), devoted to him. The poem "I'm running and standing at the crossroads" is also indebted to Loi's words. The poems in the second sequence are dedicated to Vincent Van Gogh. Those of the third sequence, to a woman ceramist whom Mancinelli met during a poetry workshop that she ran in Prato from May to September, 2019.

Diary of Passage is excerpted from *Taccuino croato* (*Croatian Notebook*), published in *Come tradurre la neve* (*How to Translate the Snow*, AnimaMundi Edizioni, 2019). The texts have resulted from the same experience evoked in *Jungle:* an itinerant creative residence which, in February 2018, brought a group of eight artists, writers, and photographers to follow, in the opposite direction, the Croatian stretch of the Balkan Route, from the Slovenian border to the Serbian border. The residence was part of the European project REFEST—Images and Words on Refugee Routes.

Many of the translated poems and prose texts, sometimes in different versions, were first published in journals and on literary websites. Our heartfelt thanks to all the editors.

Jungle first appeared in *Strands* (4 May 2020).

Master Trees was first published in *Mantis* (Spring 2021). The sequence was thereafter selected for the *Artists for Plants* project at the Svalbard Global Seed Vault in Norway in October 2022.

Several poems from the *Curved Mirror* section (the sequences *To the tiny bronze offering bearers found on Mount Titano* and *December 13th*) and from the *Three Syllables of Silence* section (the sequence *Darkroom*) appeared in a special feature devoted to Franca Mancinelli in *The Bitter Oleander* (Vol. 25, No. 2, Autumn 2019), along with an in-depth interview. Four poems from the sequence *All the Eyes that I Have Opened* appeared in an earlier issue of *The Bitter Oleander* (Vol. 24, No. 2, Autumn 2018). Excerpts from the same sequence were also published in *Journal of Italian Translation* (Vol. 13, No. 1, Spring 2018) and in *Trafika Europe 14: Italian Piazza*, 2018.

Poems from the sequence *Gleams* were published in *AzonaL* (No. 1, July-August 2020), *Osiris* (No. 90, 2020), *Bengaluru Review* (26

June 2020), *The Blue Nib* (Issue 41, April 2020), and *Right Hand Pointing* (No. 141, November 2020).

Fragments for a Dedication appeared in *Cholla Needles* (February 2021), along with the five final prose poems of this book.

Postcards for a Landscape appeared in *January Review* (Issue 3, March 2020).

Diary of Passage, under the title "from *Croatian Notebook*," was published in the *Fortnightly Review* (29 February 2020).

Franca Mancinelli was born in Fano, Italy, in 1981. She is widely considered to be one of the most compelling new poetic voices in Italian poetry. Her poems and prose poems have been translated into English by John Taylor and published at The Bitter Oleander Press: *The Little Book of Passage* (2018), *At an Hour's Sleep from Here* (2019), as well as a volume gathering her prose narratives and personal essays, *The Butterfly Cemetery* (2022). The Italian original of the present volume, *Tutti gli occhi che ho aperto* (Marcos y Marcos, 2020), has won two national prizes: the Europa in Versi Prize and the San Vito al Tagliamento Prize. With this translation, *All the Eyes that I Have Opened*, nearly all of Mancinelli's writing to date has become available in English. Taylor and Mancinelli also carry on a dialogue about literary, philosophical, and spiritual issues: the first part was published in the special feature, on her writing, in the Autumn 2019 issue of *The Bitter Oleander*; a second part appeared online in *Hopscotch Translation* (July 2021); and a third part, which was originally broadcast on Trafika Europe Radio, was published in *Eurolitkrant* (April 2022). Mancinelli has been selected for the ongoing European poetry project "Versopolis," was the Chair Poet in Residence (Calcutta, India) in January–February 2019, and participated in the European program "Refest: Images and Words on Refugee Routes" in February 2018. Her writing is also featured in the University of Oxford project "Non solo muse: panorama della poesia italiana dal 1970 a oggi," edited by Adele Bardazzi and Roberto Binetti. Her work has been translated into fifteen languages.

John Taylor was born in Des Moines in 1952. He has lived in France since 1977. Among his many translations of French, Italian, and Modern Greek literature are books by Philippe Jaccottet, Jacques Dupin, José-Flore Tappy, Pierre Voélin, Pierre Chappuis, Pierre-Albert Jourdan, Catherine Colomb, Lorenzo Calogero, Alfredo de Palchi, Elias Petropoulos, and Elias Papadimitrakopoulos. For Black Square Editions, he has translated Jaccottet's *Ponge, Pastures, Prairies*. He is the author of several volumes of short prose and poetry, most recently *The Dark Brightness* (Xenos Books, 2017), *Grassy Stairways* (The MadHat Press, 2017), *Remembrance of Water & Twenty-Five Trees* (The Bitter Oleander Press, 2018), and a "double book" coauthored with the Swiss poet Pierre Chappuis, *A Notebook of Clouds & A Notebook of Ridges* (The Fortnightly Review Press, 2018). His first two books, *The Presence of Things Past* (Story Line Press, 1992) and *Mysteries of the Body and the Mind* (Story Line Press, 1998), were republished in new editions by Red Hen Press in 2020.

Black Square Editions was started in 1999 with the intention of publishing translations of little-known books by well-known poets and fiction writers, as well as the work of emerging and established authors. After twenty-three years, we are still proceeding book by book.

Black Square Editions—a subsidiary of Off the Park Press, Inc, a tax-exempt (501c3) nonprofit organization—would like to thank the following for their support.

Tim Barry
Robert Bunker
Catherine Kehoe
Taylor Moore
Goldman Sachs
Pittsburgh Foundation Grant
Miles McEnery Gallery (New York, New York)
I.M. of Emily Mason & Wolf Kahn
Galerie Lelong & Co. (Paris, France)
Bernard Jacobson Gallery (London, England)
Saturnalia Books
& Anonymous Donors

Black Square Editions

Richard Anders *The Footprints of One Who Has Not Stepped Forth* (trans. Andrew Joron)

Andrea Applebee *Aletheia*

Eve Aschheim and Chris Daubert *Episodes with Wayne Thiebaud: Interviews*

Eve Aschheim *Eve Aschheim: Recent Work*

Anselm Berrigan *Pregrets*

Garrett Caples *The Garrett Caples Reader*

Billie Chernicoff *Minor Secrets*

Marcel Cohen *Walls (Anamneses)* (trans. Brian Evenson and Joanna Howard)

Lynn Crawford *Fortification Resort*

Lynn Crawford *Simply Separate People, Two*

Thomas Devaney *You Are the Battery*

Ming Di (Editor) *New Poetry from China: 1917–2017* (trans. various)

Joseph Donahue *Infinite Criteria*

Joseph Donahue *Red Flash on a Black Field*

Rachel Blau DuPlessis *Late Work*

Marcella Durand *To husband is to tender*

Rosalyn Drexler *To Smithereens*

Brian Evenson *Dark Property*

Jared Daniel Fagen *The Animal of Existence*

Serge Fauchereau *Complete Fiction* (trans. John Ashbery and Ron Padgett)

Jean Frémon *Painting* (trans. Brian Evenson)

Jean Frémon *The Paradoxes of Robert Ryman* (trans. Brian Evenson)

Vicente Gerbasi *The Portable Gerbasi* (trans. Guillermo Parra)

Ludwig Hohl *Ascent* (trans. Donna Stonecipher)

Isabelle Baladine Howald *phantomb* (trans. Eléna Rivera)

Philippe Jaccottet *Ponge, Pastures, Prairies* (trans. John Taylor)

Ann Jäderlund *Which once had been meadow* (trans. Johannes Göransson)

Franck André Jamme *Extracts from the Life of a Beetle* (trans. Michael Tweed)

Franck André Jamme *Another Silent Attack* (trans. Michael Tweed)

Franck André Jamme *The Recitation of Forgetting* (trans. John Ashbery)

Andrew Joron *Fathom*

Andrew Joron *OO*

Robert Kelly *Linden Word*

Karl Larsson *FORM/FORCE* (trans. Jennifer Hayashida)

Hervé Le Tellier *Atlas Inutilis* (trans. Cole Swensen)

Eugene Lim *The Strangers*

Michael Leong *Cutting Time with a Knife*

Michael Leong *Words on Edge*

Gary Lutz *I Looked Alive*

Franca Mancinelli *All the Eyes that I Have Opened* (trans. John Taylor)

Michèle Métail *Earth's Horizons: Panorama* (trans. Marcella Durand)

Michèle Métail *Identikits* (trans. Philip Terry)

Albert Mobilio *Me with Animal Towering*

Albert Mobilio *Touch Wood*

Albert Mobilio *Games & Stunts*

Albert Mobilio *Same Faces*

Pascalle Monnier *Bayart* (trans. Cole Swensen)

Christopher Nealon *The Joyous Age*

María Negroni *Berlin Interlude* (trans. Michelle Gil-Montero)

Doug Nufer *Never Again*

John Olson *Echo Regime*

John Olson *Free Stream Velocity*

Eva Kristina Olsson *The Angelgreen Sacrament* (trans. Johannes Göransson)

Juan Sánchez Peláez *Air on the Air: Selected Poems* (trans. Guillermo Parra)

Véronique Pittolo *Hero* (trans. Laura Mullen)

Pierre Reverdy *Prose Poems* (trans. Ron Padgett)

Pierre Reverdy *Haunted House* (trans. John Ashbery)

Pierre Reverdy *The Song of the Dead* (trans. Dan Bellm)

Pierre Reverdy *Georges Braque: A Methodical Adventure* (trans. Andrew Joron and Rose Vekony)

Valérie-Catherine Richez *THIS NOWHERE WHERE*

Barry Schwabsky *Book Left Open in the Rain*

Barry Schwabsky *Feelings of And*

Barry Schwabsky *Heretics of Language*

Barry Schwabsky *Trembling Hand Equilibrium*

Jeremy Sigler *Crackpot*

Jørn H. Sværen *Queen of England* (trans. Jørn H. Sværen)

Genya Turovskaya *The Breathing Body of This Thought*

Matvei Yankelevich *Some Worlds for Dr. Vogt*